# Unspoken Words

## A Child's View of Selective Mutism

By Sophia Blum

Edited by Dr. Elisa Shipon-Blum

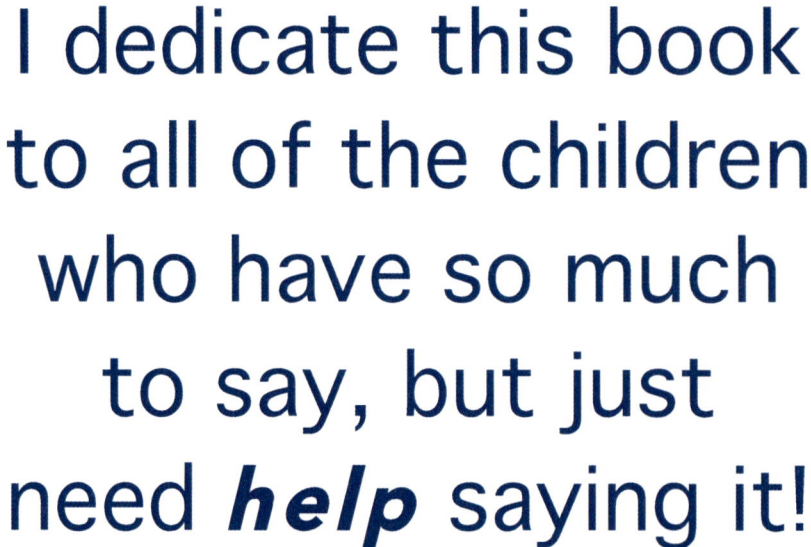

> I dedicate this book to all of the children who have so much to say, but just need *help* saying it!
>
> –Sophia Rose Blum

Unspoken Words

Text and Illustrations copyright © 2013 Sophia Blum & Dr. Elisa Shipon-Blum
www.selectivemutismcenter.org

All rights reserved. No part of this publication may be reproduced, translated, or transmitted in any form or by any means, electronic or mechanical, including photocopy, recording, or any information storage and retrieval system, without permission in writing from the publisher. For information address Dr. Elisa Shipon-Blum (www.selectivemutismcenter.org)

ISBN-13: 978-1467982597

## A note to the readers:

**For the kids** reading this book who can't get their words out, I just want you to know that I understand how you feel. As a teenager who has overcome Selective Mutism, I know that it can be scary and hard to try to get your words out. I get that it can be very upsetting when people want you to talk, but you just can't. All of the pictures in this book reflect how I felt as a kid. I know that there are things you wish that you could say, but can't use your words to explain. I tried my best to describe how you may be feeling through my pictures and words. Please know there are reasons why you feel the way you do and you are not alone. Like me, you can beat this! I hope that along with reading this book yourself, you can show this book to your family, friends, teachers, or anyone who you get scared around so that they can better understand you as well.
Good luck ☺

**For the family, teachers, friends, and professionals** reading this book, 'Unspoken Words' is just as much for you as it is for a child/teen with SM. This book is a tool for you to learn about SM, help someone suffering with SM, and even a way to help those who never experienced SM themselves better comprehend what these kids go through. It's hard, especially with a disorder that makes someone refrain from speech, to really understand what these kids are thinking and feeling. The specific situations set up in this book are my attempt at giving you a better glimpse as to what those feelings are really like because they are what went on in my mind as a kid. Hopefully this book will motivate you to continue to give your love and support to a child with SM in your life. The words in the speech bubbles are possible things that someone with SM might say or do and the thought bubbles are essentially what that kid actually means when they say it.

## Table of Contents

Unspoken Words..................................................6

My Story: Beneath My Shell........................40

My Story: From My Mom's Perspective.........53

When I say...

> I don't want to go to school today because I feel sick.

What I am trying to say is...

> I am **nervous** about something that I have to do in school today. I feel like everyone expects me to **talk**.

When I say...

> I don't like music class.

What I am trying to say is...

> The sounds of the instruments make me feel uncomfortable and I'm **expected** to play an instrument or sing with the other kids.

> **If I don't raise my hand in class,**

What I am trying to say is...

> I am too scared to let other people **hear my voice** and I don't want to make a **mistake.**

When I say...

> I don't like gym class.

What I am trying to say is...

> I get uncomfortable around a lot of kids and I'm **afraid** that I will drop the ball, **fall**, or my arms and legs feel kind of **stiff** and I can't run.

If I don't talk to my best friend at school even though I talk to her at home,

What I am trying to say is...

There are other kids and teachers around at school and I'm **uncomfortable** with *them* hearing my voice.

> If I don't go to the bathroom in school,

What I am trying to say is…

> I can't ask my teacher for permission, I don't want to bring any **attention** to myself when I get up to go or I try to go, but nothing happens.

If I don't say "Thank You" to someone when they give me a gift or say something nice to me,

What I am trying to say is...

The words are **stuck** and I feel scared or **nervous** around that person.

If I don't say "Hi" or "Bye" to our neighbors or friends,

What I am trying to say is...

I get **nervous** and I can't get the words out.

When I say...

> I don't feel well and I can't go to my friend's birthday party.

What I am trying to say is...

> I don't like **loud** and **crowded** places and I'm scared there may be people there I don't know.

## If I don't eat lunch at school,

What I am trying to say is...

The cafeteria is too loud, I can't ask for what I want, or I am too **nervous** to eat in front of the other kids.

When I say...

> I can't fall asleep at night.

What I am trying to say is...

> I am afraid to be alone, I'm scared of the dark and I **cannot calm** my thoughts.

> If I don't give my order at a restaurant,

What I am trying to say is...

> My words get stuck when I meet someone new and I feel like they are **expecting** me to talk.

When I say...

> I don't like clothes with tags and socks with thick lines by the toes.

What I am trying to say is...

> They make me feel **awkward** and itchy.

When I seem stubborn, act out, or I have a hard time with changes,

What I am trying to say is...

I feel **frustrated**, I can't explain what I am feeling and I do best with routines and when things are orderly.

If I sit alone and don't play with other kids at recess,

What I am trying to say is…

I can't ask anyone to play and I get scared feelings when I am in a **group** of people.

If it takes me a long time to do my work in school,

What I am trying to say is...

It can take me longer to think and do things when I am in school because I worry I may not get the answers right or I feel **overwhelmed**.

37

> I know that I **don't** say a lot about why I don't use my words and I may tell you that I will never speak...

But what I am trying to say is...

> I really don't know why I get so scared and the words get stuck. And I feel pressured when people ask me to talk... I really just need someone to **help** me.

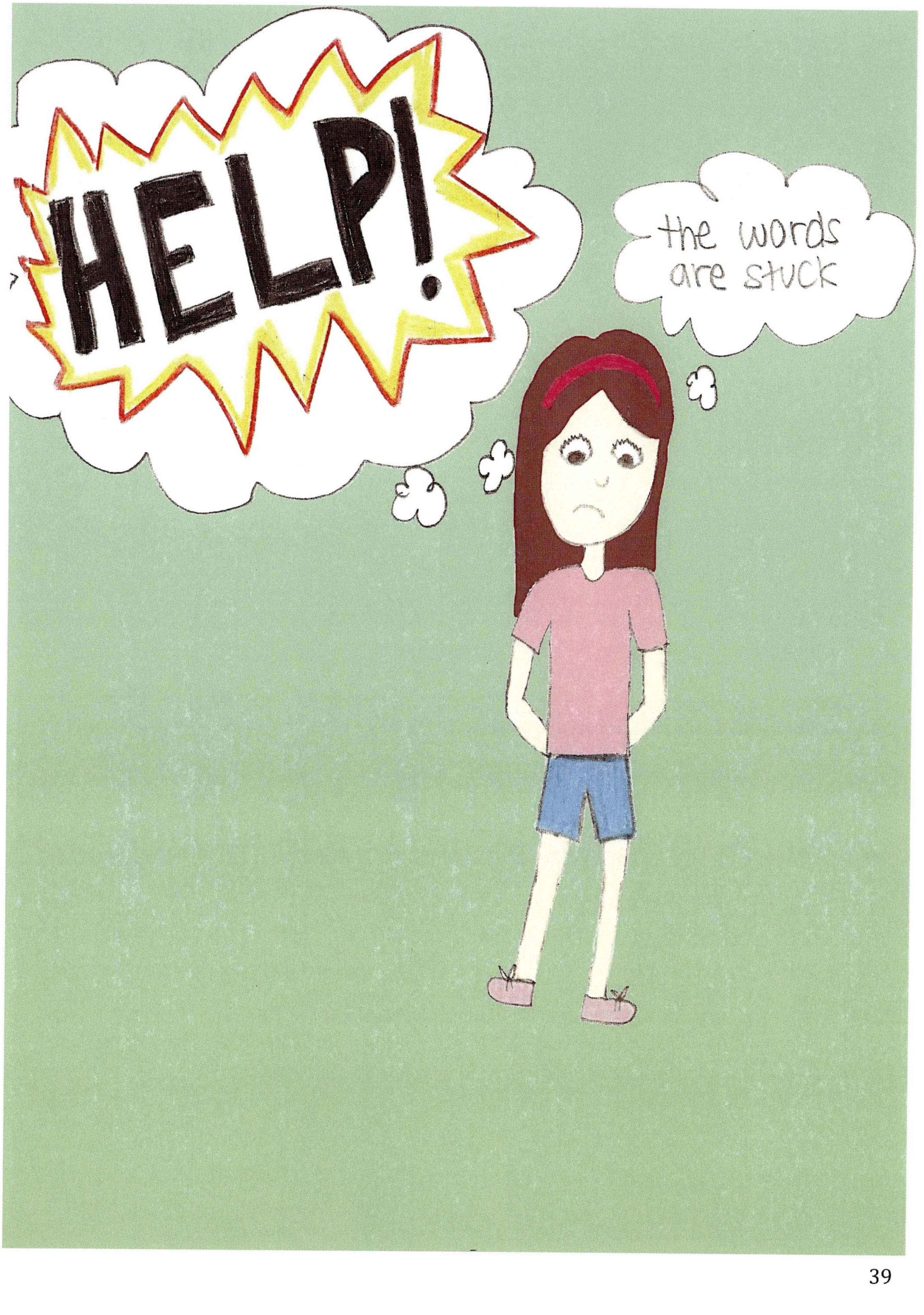
HELP!
the words are stuck

# My Story: Beneath My Shell

"Let's go around the circle and...," I froze after those words and didn't even hear what the rest of my teacher's sentence was.

"*Let's go around the circle...*"

To me, those were the most terrifying words in anyone's vocabulary. That meant everyone in the class would have to *say* something and, for a second, *everyone* would be looking at *ME*. Worse, they would be waiting for *me* to *say* something! My heart started to race to the point where I thought it might come out of my chest. I became uncomfortable, but I didn't dare move for fear that I might draw attention. The first kid in the circle answered the question. *What was the question again?* The second kid answered. My turn was quickly creeping up. *What could I do?* I was frozen with fear. I couldn't move or run away. I couldn't become invisible and sneak out of the room. It was inevitable; my turn was going to come. Soon.

*Why won't the words come out? Would it really be so bad if I talked? Everyone would stare at me! They would all be shocked if they heard my voice. What if they think that my voice is funny? It would bring too much attention to me.*

"Sophie...Sophie? It is your turn. What noise does your favorite animal make?" My teacher asked me hopefully.

I didn't move. I didn't blink. I don't even remember if I was breathing. At that point, my heart could have been beating so fast that it had stopped all together!

"Do you not know?" She sighed. "What is your favorite animal then?" She pleaded, keeping her voice calm.

My eyes shifted towards the ground. The words were on the tip of my tongue. *PUPPY*, my insides shouted, but my lips were glued shut.

Sitting in my small chair at a tiny table, I was immersed in my drawing. I loved to draw because it was one of the only ways I could express myself at school. So, when we had free time at preschool, coloring was my favorite thing to do. This day in particular, there were a few girls sitting at the table with me. Coloring was also a wonderful activity for me because it was one that you could do alone. I didn't *like* being alone, but I was too afraid to engage with anyone else. I didn't know why I was afraid, but in my five-year-old mind I knew it was weird to be afraid for people to hear my voice or to acknowledge that I existed. But I couldn't bear to break the fragile shell I put myself in during the school day. So, when Lauren, one of the girls at the table with me, asked me for the pink marker that was in my hand, I didn't respond and became motionless in the hopes that she would forget I was there. Eventually, Lauren just ended up taking the marker from my hand.

The biggest thing that I feared most of all was attention. Attention meant that I was expected to engage with others in some way, which my anxiety prevented me from doing. So, I did everything I could to remain unnoticed. Every day I wore the same kind of outfit: A pretty cotton dress with my hair pulled back by a matching headband. I also didn't allow my Mom to cut my hair short. I was afraid that if I wore something new and interesting or changed my hair too drastically, my classmates would notice the change, and the new surge of attention towards me would make school even more unbearable.

"I didn't speak today, Mommy. But I will next week," I promised.

Weeks came and went, and with them went my promises. I told my Mom that I would speak and I meant it, but when the time came to answer a question during circle time or wave hello to a classmate, I would become frozen shut again. You know that feeling in the pit of your stomach that you get right before you go onstage? Or right before you are about to go over an enormous drop on a rollercoaster? Well, that is the way I felt every day at school, but worse.

I couldn't escape my feelings. I couldn't call off the show or step out of the line. My fear followed me everywhere that I went no matter how hard I tried to conquer it. It became frustrating at times for my family and I who were all struggling to figure out what was wrong with me.

One night while my Mom was lying with me in bed; I picked up my stuffed lanky frog. But I wasn't playing with the frog. My hands were fixated on the frog's neck.

"What are you doing to the frog, Sophie?" my Mom asked me.

"I am trying to fix her voice box," I answered matter-of-factly.

"Her what?"

"The words are stuck in her voice box, Mommy. She needs surgery to get them out. Surgery will help her get the words out," I stated, picturing my own "voice box" closed shut under a lock and key.

Later, I found out that my Mom heard that I wasn't talking and interacting with my friends at school. She took me to several doctors, all of whom had no idea what was wrong with me. One of them thought that I was autistic. One said that I was just being stubborn because of bad parenting. Some thought that I should go to a "special" school. But, the worst diagnosis of all was that I was being abused at home, and that couldn't be farther from the truth. The only abuse I was getting was from myself everyday when I stepped outside of my house into the people-filled world.

When my Mom would ask me, I told her that I did play with the other kids during recess. My Mom, who watched me sit on the swings alone, was able to see the struggles that my naïve mind couldn't. In my eyes, I wasn't lying. I would sit on the swings next to some of the other kids in my class while they swung.

Back and forth they would go and I would swing, too.

Except, I wasn't swinging *with* them like I thought. I was alone. I wasn't laughing or joking around with the other kids on the swings.

I was swinging by myself.


When preschool finally ended, my Mom decided to move me to a new school. She was trying as hard as she could to help cure me of something that no one seemed to know anything about.

Even though my Mom was a doctor and she knew that the diagnoses of the specialists were all wrong, she still wasn't sure how I would react when she told me that I would be moving schools.

"I *want* to change schools, Mommy. No one will know that I don't talk there!" I cheered when I heard the great news and she looked relieved. But changing schools wasn't the only answer to my problem. My Mom knew that my condition was too severe to be cured just by a change of scenery. She helped me to understand my feelings, which helped ease the nerves. She also took me to visit the camp at my new school the summer before I started kindergarten there in the hopes that I could make some friends beforehand.

"I have a daughter who is going to be in kindergarten this year as well," Christina Jones told my Mom and I during our visit to the camp.

"That's great! Isn't it Sophie? We would love to meet her," my Mom beamed.

Mrs. Jones motioned towards the window as a group of five-year-olds were walking out of the cafeteria. "There she is now! Anna, come here. I want you to meet someone," she shouted towards her daughter.

I felt a familiar ping in my stomach as Anna

ran towards us and I hid behind my Mom's leg for protection. When she finally approached; however, I peered out from my hiding spot with a small, newfound courage. It turned out that Anna didn't seem scary to me at all. She had short brown hair and dressed like she loved to play sports.

"Hi Anna! How old are you?" My Mom asked.

"Five," Anna said holding up her hand with five extended fingers and a smile.

"Sophie is five too. Right Soph?" My Mom moved to the side in an attempt to help me engage. "When is your birthday?"

"May 12th," Anna said.

"Oh my gosh, that's Sophie's birthday too!" My Mom exclaimed as a huge smile spread across my face.

Our birthday-bond gave the necessary push that I needed for Anna and I to become fast friends, and just in time for school to start.

With preschool in my past, a new friend, and feeling more confident, I was ready to start kindergarten. I think my Mom was more nervous then I was. She was probably desperate to find out if all of her efforts would pay off at this new school. I walked through the big doors of the elementary school, keeping a solid grip on my Mom's hand. We made our way through the hallway and into the kindergarten classroom. My Mom let go of my hand and waited for me to say or do something, *anything.* I looked around the colorful room and caught a glimpse of Anna by the blocks. I smiled and turned to my Mom.

"Bye, Mommy!" I said with a wave.

The sound of my voice outside the comfort of our home stunned my Mom more than myself. She exhibited a look of shock, then relief, and then pure joy as she waved and left me to fend for myself in my new, comforting environment where I felt free to be me!

The anxiety disorder that I had, Selective Mutism(SM), was the biggest obstacle I've ever had to overcome. A lot of times when people overcome something like that, they choose to put it in their past and forget that it ever happened. But I don't see my disorder as something negative. Instead, I choose to embrace the problem that I used to have. I try to educate and help others who are just like I was, frozen with fear. I was stuck and if it weren't for my Mom, I would still be stuck to this day.

The Experience I had as a kid with Selective Mutism is what has made me who I am today. It may have been struggle, but it was worth it in order for me to end up where I am now.

# My Story: From My Mom's Perspective

Sophia, or Sophie (as we call her), was the sweetest little three-year-old who would laugh and sing out loud as she danced around our living room chanting her favorite song for the day. At bedtime Sophia would boss her lil' twin siblings around telling them to get ready for sleep while she read a book to her older brother. Sophia seemed like the happiest little angel alive!

But, unlike other children who go to school, play with other children, participate in the classroom and laugh with their friends, Sophia stood expressionless staring into space when she entered her classroom filled with children and two teachers.

Sophia rarely interacted with her school peers. She did not initiate play with other children nor did she answer the teacher's questions. She played alone in silence. During group activities, Sophia would sit in the outskirts of the group, afraid to interact. When her preschool teachers told us this about Sophia, we were so perplexed. We knew she was quiet in social situations, but we just assumed she was shy.

Days, then months and finally a year went by and still minimal interaction with her peers and no verbalization within the classroom. We kept waiting and trying different tactics to help our daughter. Within our home and in other 'comfortable' situations, Sophia was not only talkative, but she chattered nonstop! We often had to tell her to keep her voice down in order to hear the television or what someone else was saying.

But when in school, she said nothing. As the year progressed, Sophia eventually would smile, and on occasion, respond nonverbally, but she never uttered a peep.

As a medical doctor, I tried to remain objective, as a mother I was terrified and emotional. I spoke with colleagues, child psychologists, and other peers within the medical and psychological community. At first, everyone said the same thing. She is shy and will out grow this. Just relax and give her time.

But, as the next year came and went, the same scenario occurred over again.

She was completely avoidant and silent within the classroom and most social situations.

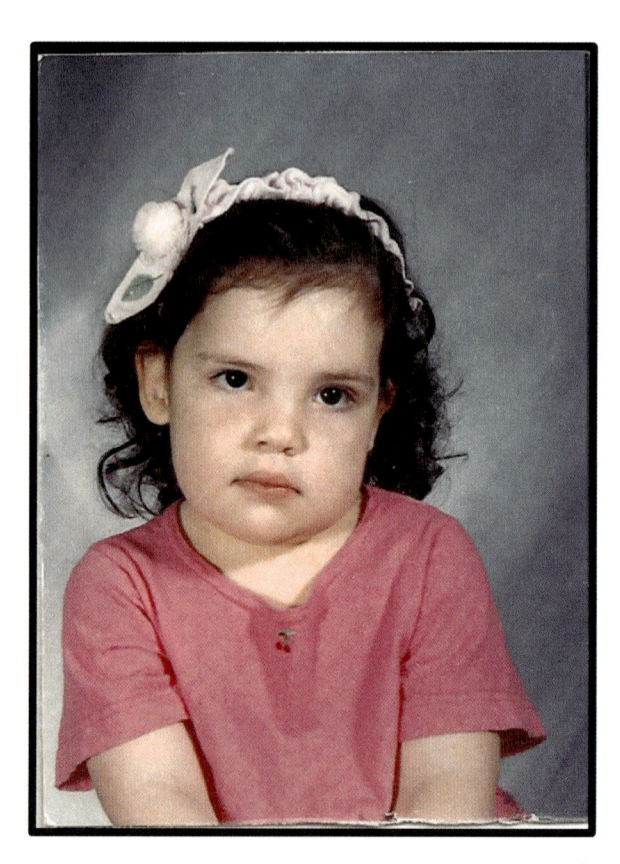

Her silence was evident at parties and family gatherings. She seemed to look forward to going to parties, but then the day would arrive and she would say she did not want to go. If she did attend, she would often 'hang' on us or hide behind us, sometimes feeling comfortable after a 'long warm up time,' usually when the party or gathering was just about over; however, she always remained mute. This caused her much frustration since when most were ready to leave; Sophia was ready to see what was going on! Yet in the market or in the mall she would chatter to us without a problem until someone approached us or asked her a question. She would then stop, become 'scared' looking and completely ignore the other person.

She would speak to a few close friends when playing at home, but was mute with most relatives and friends outside of the home.

When we discussed her 'not talking,' Sophia would just tell us, "The words just don't come out" and "I feel scared."

She would often say, "Next week Mommy, I will talk."

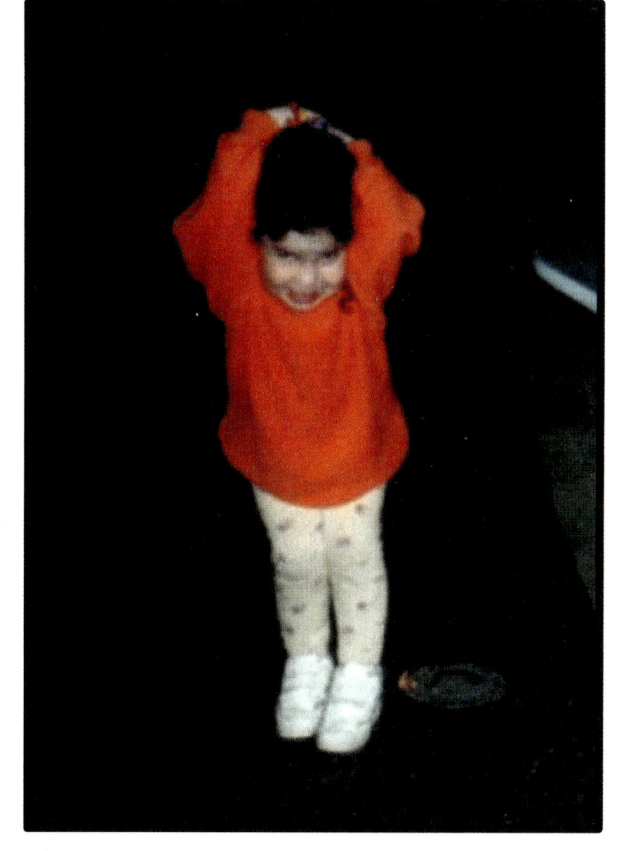

Although we never asked her to 'talk' she would often state that the words would come when she started camp or when she would go to gymnastics.

The dates that she thought she would start talking would come and go and utter silence and disappointment would be the end result of her attempts.

From reading my childhood psychiatry textbook, I found a small paragraph that seemed to describe my daughter. 'SELECTIVE MUTISM: When a child REFUSES to speak in social situations, despite the ability to speak quite normally when at home.'

Was this my daughter???? Sounded like it, but she did not seem to be REFUSING to speak. It seemed as though she was truly UNABLE to speak.

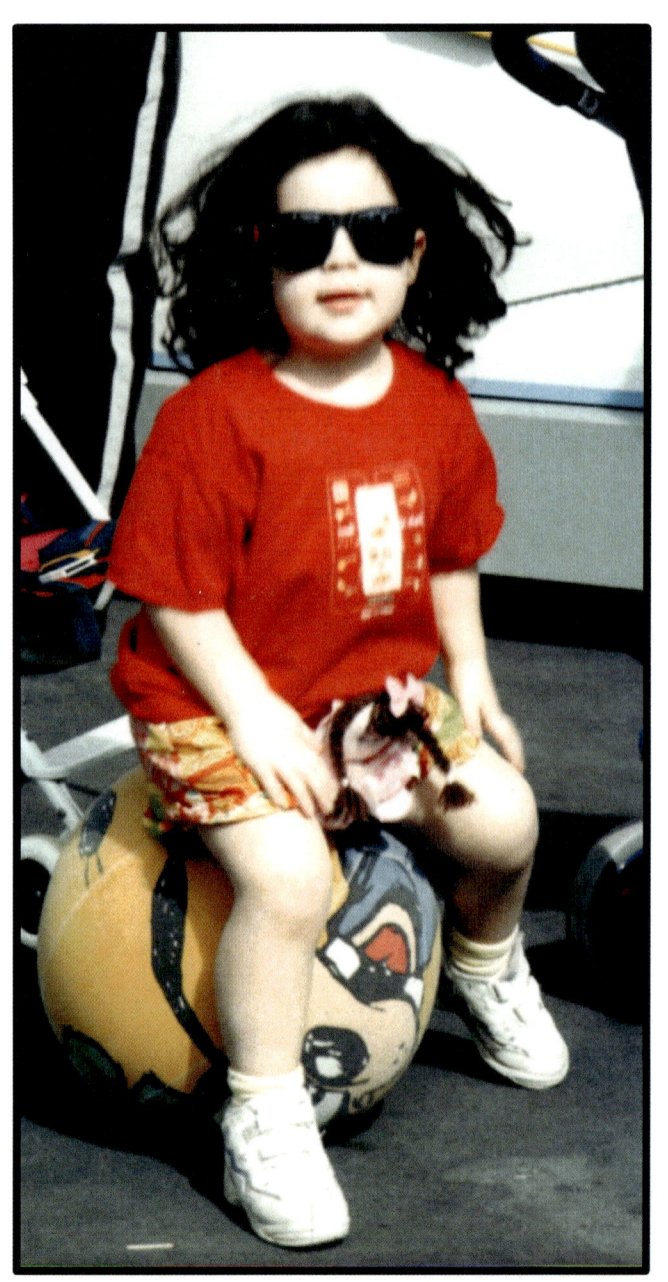

I used this term with the professionals I took my daughter to but their responses were all different. One professional told us, right in front of our incredibly perceptive child, that she was severely learning disabled and handed us literature. Another professional told us that Sophie had autism and to consider sending her to a 'special school' for kindergarten where they could address her 'special needs.' Yet, another professional told us that Sophia was purposely not speaking in order to prove a point. He suggested we withhold privileges until she speaks. Another professional implied there was 'a family secret' that we were not revealing.

Honestly, I was angry. Not one professional understood my child. I felt so helpless for Sophia!

I knew in my heart that these professionals were wrong about my child. To say I felt frustrated was an understatement.

Were these professionals describing the precocious and compassionate little girl who would run up to us and tell us how much she loved us or the child who has been reading chapter books by the time she was 3 ½ years old and then describing what she read?

Was this the little girl who refused to watch the Wizard of Oz because the bad witch was mean to Dorothy??

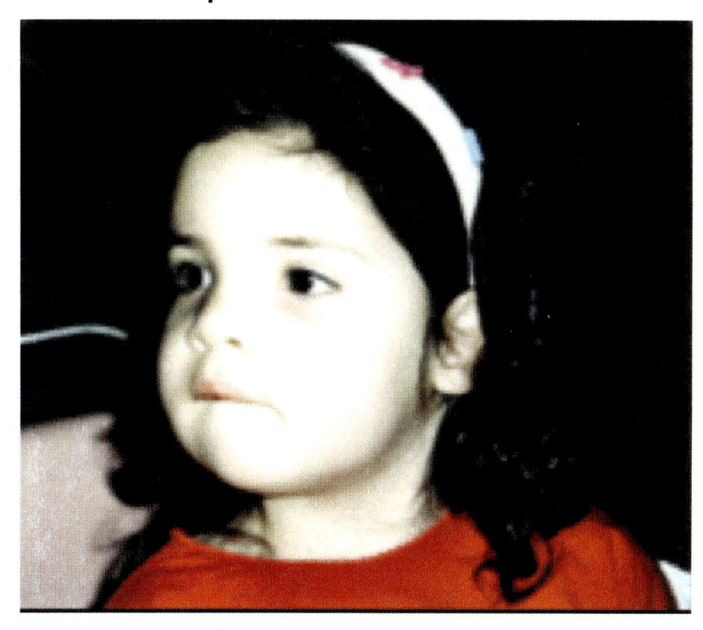

A complete paradox!

One night, while playing dolls with Sophia, I decided to do some role-playing. Using one of her dolls, I asked her why Froggy did not talk in school. Without hesitation, Sophia told the doll that Froggy wanted to talk very badly, but the words would not come out. She then started doing something to Froggy's throat. I asked her what she was doing, and she told me she was trying to operate in order to open up Froggy's voice box to let the words come out.

*I knew, then and there, that my daughter was truly suffering in silence.*

Sophie could not help her silence. Sophie was not refusing to talk or trying to show us who was boss, she was truly UNABLE to speak.

Sophia was trapped in her silence.

*This was the moment that changed my life forever.*

I was going to do whatever I could to RID THE SILENCE of this not-so understood disorder and find out all I could in order to help my child.

I gave up my then busy medical practice to focus on studying and learning all that I could about this misunderstood disorder called Selective Mutism. I soon realized that there was very little known about SM and what was known was very inconsistent and certainly did not seem to describe my daughter.

Research results, although scant, seemed to focus on subjective rather than objective findings. There were so many unanswered questions!

I read day and night. I spent days in the library researching and searching for answers. I went to every psychiatric and psychological conference I could in order to learn about the effects of fear/anxiety on the body.

I needed to know. I needed to understand!

Since I could not find a professional who could help my child, I took it upon myself to treat my then five-year-old daughter.

Since Sophie was my first true encounter with Selective Mutism, my approach was rather intuitive and 'basic' since I could not find a treatment approach that seemed to 'fit' my child's unique needs.

I felt emphasis on 'trying to get Sophia to talk' would fail and only lead to worsening anxiety and avoidant behaviors.

I devised my own treatment program consisting of various behavioral and cognitive tactics to help Sophia feel comfortable and to gain control of her 'scary' feelings in social situations.

We changed our parenting behaviors to help Sophia become more involved in a social setting yet set up the situations so that she felt safe and in control.

I worked with Sophia throughout the summer prior to the start of Kindergarten.

I had taken Sophia to the Kindergarten classroom quite often. She spent time getting to know the classroom, helping the teacher set up for the near year!  She loved to show off her toys and favorite books and before long she was able to read and then comfortably verbalize to her teacher.

I met a mom who had a daughter, Anna, who was going to be in Sophie's class. We set up play dates throughout the summer to help the girls get acquainted. They played at home and on the playground at school. Sophie and I, Anna and her teacher, spent time together in the classroom too. Sophie was able to talk to all of us in that room.

Sophia seemed so happy and comfortable!

I was cautiously optimistic about the start of Kindergarten.

The first day of Kindergarten was finally here. I walked Sophia to her classroom passing other adults and children in the hall. No sound yet. My heart was pounding in my chest. I tried so hard to smile and not let Sophia see my own internal anxiety. When I took her into the classroom, her teacher took her hand and I let go. I looked at Sophia, smiled and said, "Bye, I will see you later."

She turned to me, smiled and said in a soft voice, 'Bye, Mommy.' She walked off with the teacher.

I quietly left the room, but inside I felt as though I was truly going to explode! I wanted to scream and shout!!! I wanted to hug and kiss every person I saw and scream out to the world, "SHE SPOKE!!" My heart was pounding even harder. "SHE SPOKE, she spoke," was all I could think about.

I started to cry and I grabbed my cell phone as I walked out of the building. I called my husband and my mother and everyone else that I could think about. "SHE DID IT," was all I could manage to say, "SOPHIA TALKED!"

I knew that my little angel, who had been suffering in silence for so long, was going to be fine. She was going to be ok!!!

Throughout my dealings with my daughter, I wanted to help others so that they did not have to go through what we went through watching our child suffer in silence.

I decided to start a nonprofit organization, The Selective Mutism Group Childhood Anxiety Network (SMG~CAN), to educate and bring awareness to Selective Mutism.

From 1998, for what seemed like day/night and then day/night again, it was a nonstop effort to build a website and meet the demands of those interested in wanting information on Selective Mutism.

As the years have progressed, the organization exponentially grew. We started a membership program, which included an online newsletter, *Being Heard,* written specifically for parents of children with SM. *Ask the Doc* was started which allowed for others to ask questions and receive answers! I started *SM Connections*, a support and informational distribution program, to help others in the USA and internationally!

Families, educators, and professionals finally had resources available to them! Website hits skyrocketed as parents, school staff and treatment professionals wanted to learn as much as they could about Selective Mutism.

WOW! It was incredible to know how many other parents had children suffering and how many school staff members as well as treatment professionals were trying to find resources to help support children with Selective Mutism!

Selective Mutism is NOT rare; it is more common than autism and affects 7.1 out of 1000 children. Selective Mutism is just less known and less understood.

We have so much to do to adequately educate and promote the early diagnosis and effective treatment of children/teens who suffer in silence.

The countless e-mails and phone calls that come in every day are proof that Selective Mutism is anything but rare.

Unfortunately, what I have realized is that not only do so few know of the term, 'Selective Mutism,' but when they do, few treating professionals know how to adequately treat our children and teachers often do not know how to accommodate and provide interventions to the 'silent child' in the classroom.

To say my work is 'missionary' is true, to say the least.

*This is my purpose in life. This is my passion.*

No family or child should ever suffer the way my family and child suffered.

Although support and awareness are key in helping those affected by this crippling anxiety, a deeper understanding of Selective Mutism was needed.

I have used my medical background to gain a greater perspective on those suffering from Selective Mutism.

Understanding SM from neurodevelopmental, physiological, biochemical, genetic and environmental perspectives are necessary in order to truly understand the child suffering in silence.

I realize the importance of finding out the CAUSES as to why a child develops SM, figuring out the factors that are propagating the mutism, and then determining a proper treatment approach to help the child become a confident, social and verbal communicator at home with guests, within the real world and within the school setting.

These children have so much to offer society. They deserve to be happy, social, confident and successful! These children will NOT just grow out of their 'silence' - they need help.

They need help from their parents and teachers. They need treatment professionals who understand them. With the right support and guidance, they CAN BEAT THIS!

Children with SM are suffering... they are debilitated.

Their social-emotional development will become affected if not addressed, and many will begin to have academic challenges, not reach their academic potential while some may even leave school.

These children are not defiant and then becoming MUTE to prove a point. They are mute, avoidant and/or shut down due to the development of maladaptive coping skills to combat their anxious feelings.

As a result, these children build up defenses, and try to avoid anxiety-provoking situations. These challenging behaviors are often misunderstood as defiance and willfulness.

My passion has led to developing the **Selective Mutism Anxiety Research and Treatment Center (SMart Center)** in the northeast suburbs of Philadelphia, Pennsylvania.

As mentioned, Sophia's silence in social situations was my first encounter with Selective Mutism.

Now, 5000+ children later, I have learned so much!

I can confirm, with 100% certainty, that defiance does not cause mutism. Mutism and defensive mechanisms can cause defiance, especially when others around the child are misunderstanding his/her silence and inability to effectively socialize and communicate.

What I have learned is that the term, Selective Mutism, does not begin to touch the surface of the challenges these children endure.

I have learned that children with SM are not 'just mute' but they often have difficulty engaging socially and communicating nonverbally. Some stand motionless with fear while others look comfortable but remain silent.

I have learned to understand Selective Mutism as a **Social Communication Anxiety Disorder** and not just about 'children who do not speak.'

From the generosity of a family located in Chicago Illinois the **Selective Mutism Research Institute (SMRI)** was founded!

Their initial project was to study the treatment I developed, **Social Communication Anxiety Treatment (S-CAT)®**, which research has NOW proven to be highly effective and 'quick' for children and teens suffering with Selective Mutism.

The **Selective Mutism Stages of Social Communication Scale©** and the **Social Communication Bridge®** were both developed as part of S-CAT® to determine and illustrate a child's stage of social communication in a variety of social settings; ranging from noncommunicative (stage 0)--> nonverbal (stage 1) —> transitional (stage 2)-→ verbal communication (stage 3)

To expect a child to SPEAK when anxiety is so stifling and/or the child is so avoidant that he/she cannot even *engage* with people is a futile and frustrating way to approach children suffering in silence.

Children with SM are often 'stuck' in their silence.

Some children appear anxious, while others appear comfortable, just avoidant of speech.

Children with SM literally do not know how to 'just talk' in social settings where they sense an expectation for speech.

They need help to *transition* into speech in settings they remain mute.

We are training professionals about S-CAT® to understand SM

from a social communication perspective and a WHOLE child approach.

We work with children from around the world who suffer in silence. Some travel to the SMart Center while others consult via phone or web conference.

My staff offers time and support to parents who tell us about the pain they feel when their child sits alone, acts out at home from intense frustration or wants to drop out of school because of the profound fear they feel every time they enter school.

We travel the country to educate parents, school personnel and treating professionals via SM Conferences, training workshops, seminars, etc.

Sophie often speaks during our parent/child panel and answers questions from the audience. Sophie loves to share her experience having overcome SM.

Her goal is to offer hope to others. To let parents, teachers, treatment professionals and children know that children can indeed overcome their silence.

How rewarding to see my child on a stage and able to speak to a group of people! I would never have thought this was possible from her early years of suffering in silence.

Research is KEY to sharing my life's work with the professional community.

The good news is that it is ALL happening!

I am accomplishing my life's mission!

I have been a featured expert on national television shows such as 20/20, CNN, Inside Edition, Good Morning America as well as other local/national and international TV and Radio broadcasts.

In addition, I have been featured in TIME Magazine, People Magazine and have interviewed with newspapers such as the New York Times, Chicago Tribune, Boston Globe, San Diego Tribune, Philadelphia Inquirer, the Palm Beach Post, etc.

I get it.

I lived it!

I understand exactly what these parents are feeling and enduring.

I understand the feeling of helplessness, the pain and the desperation of witnessing your child suffering in silence as the world goes on around her.

Yet, I also know that with proper help, a child CAN indeed overcome Selective Mutism.

Sophie is happy, confident, assertive and incredibly social!

Sophie is thriving!

Sophie was co-captain of the varsity tennis team and was a leader in her high school class.

Sophie excels academically, was in all honors courses and received the all school science award in high school.

My daughter, Sophie, is now 18 years old. She graduated Abington Friends School in June 2012.

Sophie is currently attending Franklin and Marshall College (F&M).

She is in a sorority and loving college life! She is majoring in neuroscience and plans on going to medical school.

Perhaps following in her mother's footsteps? ☺

Nothing is holding Sophie back!

She is happy and enjoyed her childhood. She is thriving from a social-emotional-academic standpoint.

This is the dream that every parent wants for his/her child.

Sophia is a success story, but not everyone is as fortunate as we are.

SO much has to be done to alert the public and to teach clinicians, educators, and parents the truth about this potentially devastating childhood anxiety called Selective Mutism, where children are truly suffering in silence.

Although my daughter was the vehicle into the world of Selective Mutism, I treasure the knowledge I have acquired in the understanding and treatment of Selective Mutism.

I am eternally grateful that I can give back and can now share with others the knowledge and experience I have gained over the years.

I dream of the day when everyone understands that Selective Mutism is not about 'not speaking,' but is a Social Communication Anxiety Disorder that renders a child silent.

I dream of the day when parents, teachers and treatment professionals can recognize and address the child's social and communication difficulties when young, to enable these precious children to live their lives as happy and confident social communicators.

Written from my heart,
Sophia's mother,

Dr. Elisa Shipon-Blum

**The Selective Mutism Anxiety Research & Treatment Center (SMart Center) offers and array of services and products related to Selective Mutism!**

**SMart Center contact information:**
**Director:** Dr. Elisa Shipon-Blum
**Web:** www.selectivmutismcenter.org
**Email:** smartcenter@selectivemutismcenter.org
**Phone:** 215-887-5748 ~ **Fax:** 215-827-5722
**Address:** 505 Old York Rd. Jenkintown, PA 19046

**Services:**
--Evaluation & treatment services using the evidenced-based **Social Communication Anxiety Therapy (S-CAT)®** for children 3-20 yrs. old via in-person, telephone and web consults
--Ask the Doc consults for parents, treatment professionals and school staff seeking advice on case management, school recommendations and questions related to treatment.
-- School services: In-school child evaluations and ongoing consultation services, IEP and 504 development, staff trainings and school-based webinars
--Speech and Language evaluations and treatment for children with SM
--Professional workshops on-site and webinars!
--'Selective Mutism Conferences' around the country

**Products:** Available at the SMart Mart via www.selectivemutismcenter.org
--**Books**: Available as hard copies and E-Books:
Ideal Classroom Setting for the Selectively Mute Child
Easing School Jitters for the Selectively Mute Child
Understanding Katie (Story book about a child with SM)
Supplemental Guide to 'Understanding Guide' for Parents, Professionals & Therapists
The Selective Mutism Summer Vacation and Back to School Guide
Unspoken Words; A Child's View of Selective Mutism.
--**DVD's:**
Selective Mutism and Social Anxiety Disorder: Socializing and Communicating in the Real World (~2 hrs.)
Medication in the Treatment of Selective Mutism (~2 hrs.)
Understanding and Treating Selective Mutism as a Social Communication Anxiety Disorder (~5 hrs.)
***NEW!*** **LIVE and Prerecorded Webinars!**

Limited offer! 20% discount to purchase more products at the SMart Mart!
Go to: http://selectivemutismcenter.org/products/products Use discount code: save20now

Made in the USA
Las Vegas, NV
04 February 2022